JOSEPHINE BAKER

The Untold Story Of A Dancer, Spy, And Activist

SELENE ASHCROFT

Copyright © 2025 Selene Ashcroft All rights reserved.

This book, including its content, design, and expression, is protected by international copyright laws. Any unauthorized reproduction, distribution, adaptation, or translation of this work, in whole or in part, is strictly prohibited and may result in legal action. Permission to use or reproduce any portion of this publication must be obtained in writing from the copyright holder.

TABLE OF CONTENTS

FOREWORD 5

INTRODUCTION 28

CHAPTER ONE 35

   From St. Louis To The Stage 35

CHAPTER TWO.. 47

   Becoming The Queen Of Paris 47

CHAPTER THREE.. 62

   Josephine Baker And The Fight Against Racism 62

CHAPTER FOUR 76

   Josephine Baker And The French Resistance 76

CHAPTER FIVE 91

   A Mother To The World 91

CHAPTER SIX 104

The Comeback Josephine Baker's Return To The Stage.. 104

CHAPTER SEVEN... 109

Josephine Baker's Enduring Impact 109

FOREWORD

Josephine Baker's life defies simple categorization. She was a dancer who captivated audiences with her electrifying performances, a spy who risked her life for freedom, and an activist who fought tirelessly for equality. Her story is one of resilience, courage, and unyielding determination. Born into poverty in St. Louis, Missouri, she rose to become one of the most celebrated figures of the 20th century, breaking barriers and challenging societal norms at every turn. This biography seeks to uncover the layers of her extraordinary journey, revealing the woman behind the legend.

From her early days as a street performer to her meteoric rise in Paris, Josephine Baker redefined what it meant to be a Black woman on the global stage. Her performances were more than entertainment; they were acts of defiance against a world that sought to marginalize her. With every step, every note, and every smile, she challenged stereotypes and forced audiences to confront their prejudices. Her artistry was not just a reflection of her talent but a testament to her unshakable belief in her own worth.

Beyond the spotlight, Josephine Baker's life was marked by a deep commitment to justice. During World War II, she used her fame as a cover for her work with the French Resistance. Gathering intelligence and smuggling secrets, she became an unlikely hero in the fight against fascism. Her bravery earned her some of France's highest honors, yet her contributions often went unrecognized in her homeland. This book delves into her wartime exploits, shedding light on a chapter of her life that remains lesser-known but profoundly impactful.

Equally compelling was her role as a civil rights activist. Long before the movement gained widespread attention, Josephine Baker was using her platform to advocate for racial equality. She refused to perform for segregated audiences in the United States and worked closely with organizations like the NAACP. Her speech at the 1963 March on Washington stands as a powerful reminder of her dedication to the cause. Through her words and actions, she inspired countless others to join the fight for justice.

Josephine Baker's personal life was as unconventional as her career. Adopting twelve children from diverse backgrounds, she created her "Rainbow Tribe" as a living example of unity and harmony. Her home, Château des Milandes, became a sanctuary where love and acceptance transcended racial and cultural divides. This biography explores her vision for a better world and the challenges she faced in realizing it.

Her later years were marked by both triumph and struggle. Financial difficulties forced her to return to the stage, but she embraced the opportunity to reconnect with her audience and reaffirm her legacy. Even in the face of adversity, she remained a beacon of hope and resilience. Her story is a testament to the power of perseverance and the enduring impact of a life lived with purpose.

Josephine Baker's influence extends far beyond her lifetime. Her artistry, activism, and courage continue to inspire new generations. In 2021, she was posthumously inducted into the Panthéon in Paris, becoming the first Black woman to receive this honor. This recognition underscores the timeless relevance of her contributions and the indelible mark she left on the world.

This biography is not just a recounting of events but an exploration of the spirit that drove Josephine Baker to greatness. Through meticulous research and vivid storytelling, it seeks to capture the essence of a woman who defied expectations and changed the world. Her journey is a reminder that even in the face of overwhelming odds, one person's determination can make a profound difference.

Josephine Baker's story is one of transformation. From a young girl dancing on the streets of St. Louis to an international icon, she continually reinvented herself, refusing to be confined by the limitations imposed by others. Her life was a dance a series of movements that defied gravity and convention. Each step was a statement, each gesture a challenge to the status quo.

Her legacy is not confined to the stage or the history books. It lives on in the countless lives she touched and the barriers she shattered. She was a trailblazer, a visionary, and a force of nature. This book aims to honor her memory by telling her story in all its complexity and brilliance. It is a celebration of a life that continues to inspire and a tribute to a woman who dared to dream of a better world.

Josephine Baker's journey was not without its struggles. She faced racism, sexism, and countless obstacles on her path to success. Yet, she never allowed these challenges to define her. Instead, she used them as fuel to propel herself forward, turning adversity into opportunity. Her resilience is a lesson for us all, a reminder that greatness is not born but forged through perseverance and determination.

Her impact on the world of entertainment cannot be overstated. She revolutionized the art of performance, blending humor, sensuality, and social commentary in ways that were ahead of her time. Her influence can be seen in the work of countless artists who followed in her footsteps, from dancers to musicians to actors. She paved the way for future generations, proving that talent knows no boundaries.

Josephine Baker's activism was rooted in her own experiences of discrimination and injustice. She understood the power of her platform and used it to amplify the voices of those who were marginalized. Her commitment to equality was unwavering, and her efforts helped to lay the groundwork for the civil rights movement. This biography highlights her contributions to the fight for justice and the lasting impact of her work.

Her personal life was as vibrant and dynamic as her public life. She loved deeply, lived boldly, and embraced every moment with passion and purpose. Her relationships, both romantic and platonic, were a reflection of her boundless energy and zest for life. This book delves into the intimate details of her life, offering a glimpse into the woman behind the icon.

Josephine Baker's story is one of triumph over adversity, of light overcoming darkness. She faced countless challenges but never lost sight of her dreams. Her life is a testament to the power of resilience, the importance of standing up for what is right, and the enduring impact of a life lived with purpose. This biography seeks to capture the essence of her spirit and the legacy she left behind.

Her journey is a reminder that greatness is not defined by the absence of obstacles but by the courage to overcome them. Josephine Baker's life was a dance, a symphony, a masterpiece. She moved through the world with grace and determination, leaving an indelible mark on everyone she encountered. This book is a tribute to her extraordinary life and the lessons she continues to teach us.

Josephine Baker's legacy is one of hope, courage, and transformation. She showed us that it is possible to rise above adversity, to challenge injustice, and to create a better world. Her story is a beacon of light, guiding us toward a future defined by equality, compassion, and understanding. This biography is an invitation to explore her life, to learn from her example, and to carry her legacy forward.

In telling Josephine Baker's story, we honor not just her achievements but the spirit that drove her. She was a woman who dared to dream, who refused to be silenced, and who used her voice to uplift others. Her life is a testament to the power of resilience, the importance of standing up for what is right, and the enduring impact of a life lived with purpose. This book is a celebration of her extraordinary journey and the legacy she left behind.

Josephine Baker's life was a tapestry of triumphs and trials, of joy and sorrow, of love and loss. She was a woman of contradictions, defying easy categorization and challenging the world to see her for who she truly was. Her story is one of courage, creativity, and unwavering determination. This biography seeks to capture the essence of her spirit and the legacy she left behind.

Her impact on the world cannot be overstated. She was a trailblazer, a visionary, and a force of nature. Her life was a dance a series of movements that defied gravity and convention. Each step was a statement, each gesture a challenge to the status quo. This book is a tribute to her extraordinary life and the lessons she continues to teach us.

Josephine Baker's story is one of transformation. From a young girl dancing on the streets of St. Louis to an international icon, she continually reinvented herself, refusing to be confined by the limitations imposed by others. Her life was a dance a series of movements that defied gravity and convention. Each step was a statement, each gesture a challenge to the status quo.

Her legacy is not confined to the stage or the history books. It lives on in the countless lives she touched and the barriers she shattered. She was a trailblazer, a visionary, and a force of nature. This book aims to honor her memory by telling her story in all its complexity and brilliance. It is a celebration of a life that continues to inspire and a tribute to a woman who dared to dream of a better world.

Josephine Baker's journey was not without its struggles. She faced racism, sexism, and countless obstacles on her path to success. Yet, she never allowed these challenges to define her. Instead, she used them as fuel to propel herself forward, turning adversity into opportunity. Her resilience is a lesson for us all, a reminder that greatness is not born but forged through perseverance and determination.

Her impact on the world of entertainment cannot be overstated. She revolutionized the art of performance, blending humor, sensuality, and social commentary in ways that were ahead of her time. Her influence can be seen in the work of countless artists who followed in her footsteps, from dancers to musicians to actors. She paved the way for future generations, proving that talent knows no boundaries.

Josephine Baker's activism was rooted in her own experiences of discrimination and injustice. She understood the power of her platform and used it to amplify the voices of those who were marginalized. Her commitment to equality was unwavering, and her efforts helped to lay the groundwork for the civil rights movement. This biography highlights her contributions to the fight for justice and the lasting impact of her work.

Her personal life was as vibrant and dynamic as her public persona. She loved deeply, lived boldly, and embraced every moment with passion and purpose. Her relationships, both romantic and platonic, were a reflection of her boundless energy and zest for life. This book delves into the intimate details of her life, offering a glimpse into the woman behind the icon.

Josephine Baker's story is one of triumph over adversity, of light overcoming darkness. She faced countless challenges but never lost sight of her dreams. Her life is a testament to the power of resilience, the importance of standing up for what is right, and the enduring impact of a life lived with purpose. This biography seeks to capture the essence of her spirit and the legacy she left behind.

Her journey is a reminder that greatness is not defined by the absence of obstacles but by the courage to overcome them. Josephine Baker's life was a dance, a symphony, a masterpiece. She moved through the world with grace and determination, leaving an indelible mark on everyone she encountered. This book is a tribute to her extraordinary life and the lessons she continues to teach us.

Josephine Baker's legacy is one of hope, courage, and transformation. She showed us that it is possible to rise above adversity, to challenge injustice, and to create a better world. Her story is a beacon of light, guiding us toward a future defined by equality, compassion, and understanding. This biography is an invitation to explore her life, to learn from her example, and to carry her legacy forward.

In telling Josephine Baker's story, we honor not just her achievements but the spirit that drove her. She was a woman who dared to dream, who refused to be silenced, and who used her voice to uplift others. Her life is a testament to the power of resilience, the importance of standing up for what is right, and the enduring impact of a life lived with purpose. This book is a celebration of her extraordinary journey and the legacy she left behind.

Josephine Baker's life was a tapestry of triumphs and trials, of joy and sorrow, of love and loss. She was a woman of contradictions, defying easy categorization and challenging the world to see her for who she truly was. Her story is one of courage, creativity, and unwavering determination. This biography seeks to capture the essence of her spirit and the legacy she left behind.

Her impact on the world cannot be overstated. She was a trailblazer, a visionary, and a force of nature. Her life was a dance a series of movements that defied gravity and convention. Each step was a statement, each gesture a challenge to the status quo. This book is a tribute to her extraordinary life and the lessons she continues to teach us.

Josephine Baker's story is one of transformation. From a young girl dancing on the streets of St. Louis to an international icon, she continually reinvented herself, refusing to be confined by the limitations imposed by others. Her life was a dance a series of movements that defied gravity and convention. Each step was a statement, each gesture a challenge to the status quo.

Her legacy is not confined to the stage or the history books. It lives on in the countless lives she touched and the barriers she shattered. She was a trailblazer, a visionary, and a force of nature. This book aims to honor her memory by telling her story in all its complexity and brilliance. It is a celebration of a life that continues to inspire and a tribute to a woman who dared to dream of a better world.

Josephine Baker's journey was not without its struggles. She faced racism, sexism, and countless obstacles on her path to success. Yet, she never allowed these challenges to define her. Instead, she used them as fuel to propel herself forward, turning adversity into opportunity. Her resilience is a lesson for us all, a reminder that greatness is not born but forged through perseverance and determination.

Her impact on the world of entertainment cannot be overstated. She revolutionized the art of performance, blending humor, sensuality, and social commentary in ways that were ahead of her time. Her influence can be seen in the work of countless artists who followed in her footsteps, from dancers to musicians to actors. She paved the way for future generations, proving that talent knows no boundaries.

Josephine Baker's activism was rooted in her own experiences of discrimination and injustice. She understood the power of her platform and used it to amplify the voices of those who were marginalized. Her commitment to equality was unwavering, and her efforts helped to lay the groundwork for the civil rights movement. This biography highlights her contributions to the fight for justice and the lasting impact of her work.

Her personal life was as vibrant and dynamic as her public persona. She loved deeply, lived boldly, and embraced every moment with passion and purpose. Her relationships, both romantic and platonic, were a reflection of her boundless energy and zest for life. This book delves into the intimate details of her life, offering a glimpse into the woman behind the icon.

Josephine Baker's story is one of triumph over adversity, of light overcoming darkness. She faced countless challenges but never lost sight of her dreams. Her life is a testament to the power of resilience, the importance of standing up for what is right, and the enduring impact of a life lived with purpose. This biography seeks to capture the essence of her spirit and the legacy she left behind.

Her journey is a reminder that greatness is not defined by the absence of obstacles but by the courage to overcome them. Josephine Baker's life was a dance, a symphony, a masterpiece. She moved through the world with grace and determination, leaving an indelible mark on everyone she encountered. This book is a tribute to her extraordinary life and the lessons she continues to teach us.

Josephine Baker's legacy is one of hope, courage, and transformation. She showed us that it is possible to rise above adversity, to challenge injustice, and to create a better world. Her story is a beacon of light, guiding us toward a future defined by equality, compassion, and understanding. This biography is an invitation to explore her life, to learn from her example, and to carry her legacy forward.

In telling Josephine Baker's story, we honor not just her achievements but the spirit that drove her. She was a woman who dared to dream, who refused to be silenced, and who used her voice to uplift others. Her life is a testament to the power of resilience, the importance of standing up for what is right, and the enduring impact of a life lived with purpose. This book is a celebration of her extraordinary journey and the legacy she left behind.

Josephine Baker's life was a tapestry of triumphs and trials, of joy and sorrow, of love and loss. She was a woman of contradictions, defying easy categorization and challenging the world to see her for who she truly was. Her story is one of courage, creativity, and unwavering determination. This biography seeks to capture the essence of her spirit and the legacy she left behind.

Her impact on the world cannot be overstated. She was a trailblazer, a visionary, and a force of nature. Her life was a dance a series of movements that defied gravity and convention. Each step was a statement, each gesture a challenge to the status quo. This book is a tribute to her extraordinary life and the lessons she continues to teach us.

Josephine Baker's story is one of transformation. From a young girl dancing on the streets of St. Louis to an international icon, she continually reinvented herself, refusing to be confined by the limitations imposed by others. Her life was a dance a series of movements that defied gravity and convention. Each step was a statement, each gesture a challenge to the status quo.

Her legacy is not confined to the stage or the history books. It lives on in the countless lives she touched and the barriers she shattered. She was a trailblazer, a visionary, and a force of nature. This book aims to honor her memory by telling her story in all its complexity and brilliance. It is a celebration of a life that continues to inspire and a tribute to a woman who dared to dream of a better world.

Josephine Baker's journey was not without its struggles. She faced racism, sexism, and countless obstacles on her path to success. Yet, she never allowed these challenges to define her. Instead, she used them as fuel to propel herself forward, turning adversity into opportunity. Her resilience is a lesson for us all, a reminder that greatness is not born but forged through perseverance and determination.

Her impact on the world of entertainment cannot be overstated. She revolutionized the art of performance, blending humor, sensuality, and social commentary in ways that were ahead of her time. Her influence can be seen in the work of countless artists who followed in her footsteps, from dancers to musicians to actors. She paved the way for future generations, proving that talent knows no boundaries.

Josephine Baker's activism was rooted in her own experiences of discrimination and injustice. She understood the power of her platform and used it to amplify the voices of those who were marginalized. Her commitment to equality was unwavering, and her efforts helped to lay the groundwork for the civil rights movement. This biography highlights her contributions to the fight for justice and the lasting impact of her work.

Her personal life was as vibrant and dynamic as her public persona. She loved deeply, lived boldly, and embraced every moment with passion and purpose. Her relationships, both romantic and platonic, were a reflection of her boundless energy and zest for life.

INTRODUCTION

Josephine Baker's life was a symphony of courage, creativity, and defiance. She was a dancer who mesmerized audiences, a spy who risked her life for freedom, and an activist who fought tirelessly for equality. Her story transcends time, offering lessons in resilience, artistry, and the power of standing up for what is right. This biography invites you to explore the untold stories behind her legendary life, revealing the woman behind the icon.

Each chapter of this book focuses on a distinct phase of Josephine Baker's journey, offering a deeper understanding of her multifaceted legacy. From her humble beginnings in St. Louis to her rise as a global superstar, her daring work as a spy during World War II, and her unwavering commitment to civil rights, this biography uncovers the layers of her extraordinary life. Here's a glimpse of what awaits you in the pages ahead.

Josephine Baker's story begins in the impoverished streets of St. Louis, Missouri. Born into a world of hardship, she discovered her love for dance as a child, performing on street corners for spare change. This chapter traces her early years, from her work as a domestic helper to her first steps into vaudeville. Readers will witness the resilience and determination that propelled her from poverty to the bright lights of the stage.

In 1925, Josephine Baker arrived in Paris and quickly became a sensation. Her performances at the Théâtre des Champs-Élysées, including the iconic "Banana Dance," redefined entertainment and made her a symbol of the Jazz Age. This chapter explores her meteoric rise to fame, her impact on Parisian culture, and how she used her art to challenge societal norms.

Josephine Baker's fame gave her a platform, and she used it to confront racial injustice. Refusing to perform for segregated audiences in the United

States, she became a vocal advocate for civil rights. This chapter delves into her work with organizations like the NAACP and her efforts to combat racism both at home and abroad.

During World War II, Josephine Baker traded the stage for the shadows, becoming a spy for the French Resistance. Using her celebrity status as a cover, she gathered intelligence and smuggled secrets, risking her life for the cause of freedom. This chapter uncovers her wartime exploits and the bravery that earned her France's highest honors.

Josephine Baker's vision of a better world extended beyond her performances and activism. Adopting twelve children from diverse backgrounds, she created her "Rainbow Tribe" as a living example of unity and harmony. This chapter explores her role as a mother, her life at Château des Milandes, and the challenges she faced in realizing her dream of a global family.

Financial difficulties forced Josephine Baker to return to the stage in the 1950s and 1960s, but she embraced the opportunity to reconnect with her audience and reaffirm her legacy. This chapter delves into her later career, from her triumphant performances to her continued activism during the civil rights movement.

Josephine Baker's influence extends far beyond her lifetime. Her artistry, activism, and courage continue to inspire new generations. This chapter reflects on her lasting legacy, from her induction into the Panthéon in Paris to the countless lives she touched through her work. Her story is a testament to the power of resilience and the enduring impact of a life lived with purpose.

This biography is more than a recounting of events; it is an exploration of the spirit that drove Josephine Baker to greatness. Through meticulous research and vivid storytelling, it seeks to capture the essence of a woman who defied expectations and changed the world. Her journey is a reminder that even in the face of overwhelming odds, one person's determination can make a profound difference.

Josephine Baker's life was a dance a series of movements that defied gravity and convention. Each step was a statement, each gesture a challenge to the status quo. Her legacy is not confined to the stage or the history books. It lives on in the countless lives she touched and the barriers she shattered. She was a trailblazer, a visionary, and a force of nature.

This book aims to honor her memory by telling her story in all its complexity and brilliance. It is a celebration of a life that continues to inspire and a tribute to a woman who dared to dream of a better world. Her journey is a reminder that greatness is not defined by the absence of obstacles but by the courage to overcome them.

In telling Josephine Baker's story, we honor not just her achievements but the spirit that drove her. She was a woman who dared to dream, who refused to be silenced, and who used her voice to uplift others. Her life is a testament to the power of resilience, the importance of standing up for what is right, and the enduring impact of a life lived with purpose. This book is a celebration of her extraordinary journey and the legacy she left behind.

Her impact on the world cannot be overstated. She was a trailblazer, a visionary, and a force of nature. Her life was a dance a series of movements that defied gravity and convention. Each step was a statement, each gesture a challenge to the status quo. This book is a tribute to her extraordinary life and the lessons she continues to teach us.

Josephine Baker's story is one of transformation. From a young girl dancing on the streets of St. Louis to an international icon, she continually reinvented herself, refusing to be confined by the limitations imposed by others. Her life was a dance a series of movements that defied gravity and convention. Each step was a statement, each gesture a challenge to the status quo.

CHAPTER ONE

From St. Louis To The Stage

Josephine Baker's story begins on June 3, 1906, in St. Louis, Missouri. Born Freda Josephine McDonald, she came into the world under the shadow of poverty. Her mother, Carrie McDonald, was a washerwoman and former dancer who harbored dreams of the stage that her circumstances couldn't allow her to pursue. Josephine's father, Eddie Carson, was a drummer who abandoned the family early, leaving Carrie to raise Josephine and her three siblings alone. Life was a constant struggle, and young Josephine grew up acutely aware of the challenges that defined her family's existence.

The McDonald household was no stranger to deprivation. They lived in the Mill Creek Valley neighborhood, a densely packed area rife with poverty and systemic racism. The family resided in a small, ramshackle house with barely enough room for all of them. Hunger was a constant companion, and Josephine often scavenged for food in garbage bins or depended on the generosity of neighbors to make it through the day.

Despite the hardships, Josephine was a curious and spirited child. Her laughter often filled the air, masking the adversity she faced. She developed a mischievous streak and a flair for storytelling, traits that hinted at the performer she would later become. However, her childhood was not without moments of harsh reality. Racial segregation and discrimination were rampant in St. Louis, and Josephine experienced the sting of bigotry firsthand. These early encounters with inequality would later fuel her determination to challenge societal norms.

By the age of eight, Josephine began working as a domestic helper for white families. The work was grueling, and she faced harsh treatment from her employers, who often reminded her of her place in the racial hierarchy. These early jobs exposed Josephine to the indignities of servitude, but they also taught her resilience and adaptability.

When she wasn't working, Josephine found solace in the bustling streets of St. Louis. She was drawn to the sounds of music and laughter emanating from the vibrant black community. By the time she was a teenager, she was performing street dances to earn spare change. Her antics, which included contorting her face into exaggerated expressions and improvising comic dances, quickly made her a local favorite.

At 13, Josephine's life took a dramatic turn when she joined the Jones Family Band and the Dixie Steppers, two local vaudeville troupes. This marked her first formal step into the world of performance. Although she started as a dresser for the troupes, her undeniable talent soon earned her a place on the stage. Her comedic timing and knack for physical comedy set her apart.

Josephine's big break came when she was cast in the chorus line for a touring vaudeville show. Her role was modest, but her presence on stage was electric. She quickly became known for her ability to bring energy and humor to every performance. Audiences adored her, and she began to develop the bold, uninhibited style that would later become her trademark.

The streets of St. Louis played a significant role in shaping Josephine's artistic sensibilities. The city was a melting pot of musical styles, including blues, ragtime, and jazz. Josephine absorbed these influences and incorporated them into her performances. Her unique blend of dance, music, and comedy was a reflection of the cultural richness of her hometown, even as she yearned to escape its confines.

At the age of 15, Josephine left St. Louis and moved to New York City, determined to make a name for herself. She arrived during the Harlem Renaissance, a cultural movement that celebrated black artistry and creativity. New York offered opportunities that St. Louis could not, and Josephine quickly immersed herself in the vibrant theater scene.

She secured a spot in the chorus of Shuffle Along, a groundbreaking all-black musical that became a Broadway sensation. Josephine's role was initially small, but her energetic dancing and knack for improvisation soon caught the attention of audiences and producers alike. She became known for her "rubber-legged" dance moves and her ability to captivate a crowd.

Josephine Baker's childhood was marked by more than just poverty it was defined by her relentless spirit to rise above her circumstances. Despite facing hunger and harsh working conditions, she had an innate ability to turn life's difficulties into moments of joy. Josephine entertained her siblings and neighbors with her inventive dances and exaggerated facial expressions. Her performances were not just an escape for herself but also for the people around her who lived similar lives of struggle.

Josephine's family life was a source of both support and tension. Her mother, Carrie, hoped that Josephine would pursue a stable and traditional path, working as a domestic helper to contribute to the family. However, Josephine had other plans. Even as a child, she dreamed of a life on stage, captivated by the idea of performing for audiences who would cheer her on. This dream was fueled by the music and culture that permeated the black community in St. Louis, particularly in the bustling area of Market Street, where jazz and blues echoed from local bars and clubs.

While Josephine's dreams clashed with her mother's practical aspirations, they also gave her a reason to endure. She often used her earnings from domestic work to attend local performances, sneaking into theaters when she could. These early glimpses of professional performers inspired her to believe that a life beyond St. Louis was possible, even if it seemed far out of reach.

Growing up in the segregated South, Josephine was exposed to the harsh realities of systemic racism from a young age. She witnessed race riots, including the infamous East St. Louis riots of 1917, which left a deep scar on her community. These events exposed her to the violence and prejudice that black people endured daily. The riots would later influence Josephine's commitment to activism and her refusal to accept racial inequality, but as a child, they were terrifying reminders of her place in a deeply divided society.

Even in her early performances on the streets of St. Louis, Josephine encountered resistance. Many viewed her antics as too bold or unconventional, particularly for a young black girl. However, Josephine's confidence never wavered. She used criticism as motivation, constantly refining her craft and adding new elements to her street performances to captivate onlookers. She learned how to command attention in any setting, a skill that would serve her well throughout her career.

Josephine's first exposure to professional dance came through vaudeville, but her love for movement began long before that. As a child, she would mimic the dance styles she observed in her community, combining traditional steps with her own improvisations. Her natural rhythm and ability to invent unique movements set her apart, even before she received any formal training.

Her early work in vaudeville troupes introduced her to a more structured form of performance. She learned the importance of timing, choreography, and working within an ensemble. However, Josephine was never one to blend into the background. Even as a chorus girl, she found ways to stand out, often adding her signature comedic touches to routines. This tendency to innovate sometimes frustrated her directors, but audiences adored her for it.

Leaving St. Louis was not an easy decision for Josephine. She was barely 15 years old, and the idea of moving to New York was both thrilling and daunting. However, she knew that staying in St. Louis would mean a life of limited opportunities. With her sights set on bigger stages, she joined a traveling vaudeville troupe that eventually brought her to the city that would change her life.

When Josephine arrived in New York, she was overwhelmed by the sheer scale of the city. The lights of Broadway, the bustling streets of Harlem, and the rich cultural scene offered endless possibilities. However, breaking into the New York theater world was no small feat, especially for a young black woman with limited formal training.

Josephine began by auditioning for chorus lines and small roles in local productions. She faced rejection after rejection, but her determination never faltered. She spent her days rehearsing tirelessly, studying the movements of more experienced dancers, and absorbing the energy of the Harlem Renaissance. The cultural explosion of the era gave Josephine a sense of belonging and fueled her ambition to succeed.

One of the key moments in Josephine's early New York career came when she auditioned for Shuffle Along. The musical was a groundbreaking production that showcased the talents of black performers and brought jazz to the Broadway stage.

For Josephine, securing a role in the chorus was a dream come true.

However, her time in Shuffle Along was not without its challenges. Josephine often felt overshadowed by more established performers, and the pressure to conform to the show's strict choreography was stifling. Still, she found ways to make her mark. During one performance, she deliberately fumbled her steps and turned the mistake into a comedic bit. The audience roared with laughter, and Josephine realized the power of improvisation. From that point on, she began to infuse her performances with her unique style, turning potential failures into moments of triumph.

Josephine's time in New York was transformative. She honed her craft, developed her unique style, and began to envision a future beyond the chorus line. She also witnessed the struggles of black performers in a segregated industry, which deepened her commitment to breaking barriers.

By the time she was 19, Josephine Baker had established herself as a rising star in the New York theater scene. She was no longer the impoverished girl from St. Louis scavenging for food; she was a performer with a vision. Her early struggles had taught her the value of perseverance, and her experiences in vaudeville and on the streets of St. Louis had given her the tools she needed to succeed.

CHAPTER TWO

Becoming The Queen Of Paris

Josephine Baker's decision to leave the United States in 1925 marked a turning point that would define her legacy. While she had achieved moderate success in New York, racial prejudice and limited opportunities prevented her from reaching her full potential. Paris offered a fresh start, a place where artistry and individuality were celebrated, and where Josephine could become not just a performer, but a sensation.

Josephine arrived in Paris as part of the cast of La Revue Nègre, a show created to introduce African-American culture, jazz, and dance to European audiences. The Paris of the 1920s was alive with artistic experimentation and an openness to new ideas, making it the perfect stage for Josephine to thrive. The city had become a magnet for creatives, intellectuals, and free spirits, and the Jazz Age was in full swing. Parisian audiences were eager for fresh and bold expressions of art, and La Revue Nègre promised just that.

Josephine's introduction to Parisian audiences came at the Théâtre des Champs-Élysées, a venue known for avant-garde performances. On opening night, the audience, including the city's elite, was unsure of what to expect. What they saw exceeded their wildest imaginations. Josephine stepped onto the stage with a confidence and charisma that captivated the crowd from the moment the music began.

The performance that launched Josephine into the international spotlight was the now-iconic "Banana Dance." Wearing a skirt made of artificial bananas and little else, Josephine combined frenetic energy with an unmistakable sense of humor, charm, and sensuality. The dance was provocative but playful, a celebration of rhythm and movement that showcased Josephine's uninhibited approach to performance.

The costume, designed by Paul Colin, became a symbol of Josephine's persona: bold, exotic, and unforgettable. It was a deliberate departure from traditional European aesthetics, embracing elements of African and Caribbean culture in a way that both fascinated and shocked Parisian audiences. While the performance was criticized by some as reinforcing racial stereotypes, Josephine reclaimed those elements and infused them with power, agency, and artistry.

The success of the Banana Dance cemented Josephine's status as the star of La Revue Nègre. Critics raved about her magnetic stage presence, describing her as a force of nature. Paris had never seen anything like her, and Josephine's performances became the talk of the city.

Josephine quickly became synonymous with the Jazz Age, a time defined by a celebration of freedom, creativity, and rebellion against societal norms. Her performances embodied the spirit of the era, blending jazz music with daring choreography and an unapologetic embrace of individuality.

Beyond her onstage persona, Josephine became a fixture in Parisian social circles. She befriended artists, writers, and intellectuals, including Pablo Picasso, Ernest Hemingway, and Langston Hughes. Her magnetic personality drew people to her, and she was admired not just for her talent, but for her courage and authenticity.

Josephine's rise to fame also coincided with the emergence of jazz as a global phenomenon. Her performances introduced European audiences to the rhythms and sounds of African-American music, further solidifying her role as a cultural ambassador. She worked closely with musicians such as Sidney Bechet and Claude Hopkins, who helped her craft a sound that was both innovative and true to her roots.

As Josephine's fame grew, so did her opportunities. After the success of La Revue Nègre, she was offered a contract to perform at the Folies Bergère, one of Paris's most prestigious venues. Her shows at the Folies Bergère were grand spectacles, blending music, dance, and elaborate costumes to create an experience unlike anything audiences had ever seen.

Josephine was not just a dancer; she was a storyteller. Each performance was carefully choreographed to evoke emotion and tell a narrative, whether it was one of joy, desire, or empowerment. Her ability to connect with audiences on an emotional level set her apart from other performers and solidified her reputation as a true artist.

Josephine's success in Paris was groundbreaking not only for her as an individual but for African-American performers as a whole. At a time when racial discrimination was rampant in the United States, Josephine was celebrated in France for her talent and individuality. She became a symbol of progress and possibility, showing that it was possible to achieve greatness despite the barriers of race and class.

However, Josephine was not blind to the complexities of her position. While she was adored in Paris, she remained acutely aware of the stereotypes that shaped European perceptions of black performers. Rather than shy away from these challenges, Josephine confronted them head-on, using her art to challenge and redefine those perceptions. Her performances were both a celebration of black culture and a reclamation of her identity, blending humor, defiance, and artistry to create something entirely her own.

Josephine's time in Paris was not just a period of professional success; it was also a time of personal growth. Freed from the constraints of American society, she embraced her individuality and explored new facets of her identity. She experimented with fashion, adopting bold and unconventional styles that would later influence the worlds of design and haute couture.

Her newfound freedom also allowed her to explore her sexuality openly. Josephine had relationships with both men and women, and her confidence in embracing her desires was ahead of its time. This openness further endeared her to her Parisian audience, who saw her as a symbol of liberation and self-expression.

As the 1920s progressed, Josephine's star continued to rise. She toured across Europe, performing in cities such as Berlin, Vienna, and London, where she was met with the same adoration she had found in Paris. Each performance was a celebration of life, music, and movement, and Josephine's ability to adapt to different audiences made her a truly global star.

Josephine's influence extended beyond the stage. She became a muse for artists such as Alexander Calder and Jean Cocteau, who were captivated by her energy and originality. Her image was immortalized in paintings, sculptures, and posters, ensuring that her legacy would endure long after the music stopped.

Following the runaway success of the Banana Dance, Josephine Baker continued to evolve her artistry. She was determined not to be a one-dimensional performer and set out to expand her repertoire. At the Folies Bergère, Josephine introduced new routines that pushed creative boundaries. One of her most famous performances featured her emerging from a giant, illuminated shell, covered in shimmering jewels and pearls. The act was not only a visual masterpiece but a declaration of her status as an entertainer who had transcended ordinary stardom.

Her ability to integrate storytelling into her performances kept audiences captivated. Each dance was meticulously designed to convey an emotion or idea. One particularly moving routine, inspired by her childhood, saw her dancing barefoot in a simple dress, juxtaposing her humble beginnings with her Parisian triumph. She wanted her audience to understand that while she had risen to fame, she had never forgotten where she came from.

Josephine also began incorporating different musical styles into her shows. While jazz remained her cornerstone, she experimented with classical elements, African drum beats, and Latin rhythms. This musical diversity enhanced her performances and set her apart as an artist who was unafraid to explore uncharted territories.

Josephine Baker wasn't just a performer; she became a cultural icon, adored by people across Europe. Her face appeared on posters, in magazines, and on postcards. She lent her name to various commercial products, including perfumes and cosmetics, further cementing her status as a household name.

Her influence extended far beyond the stage. Fashion designers clamored to dress her, and she became a trendsetter in her own right. Her sleek, short haircut known as the "Eton crop" became a sensation, with women across Europe imitating her daring style. Designers such as Jean Patou and Elsa Schiaparelli were inspired by Josephine's boldness, creating looks that captured the spirit of the Jazz Age and her vivacious personality.

As Josephine's fame grew, so did her wealth. She purchased a luxurious apartment in the heart of Paris and hosted extravagant parties that drew some of the most influential people of the time. Writers, painters, and musicians mingled at her soirées, and Josephine's charm made her the center of attention.

Despite her immense popularity, Josephine's career in Europe was not without controversy. Critics accused her performances of being too provocative, and some questioned the authenticity of her depictions of African culture. While many saw her routines as celebrations of African heritage, others argued they perpetuated colonial stereotypes.

Josephine was aware of these criticisms and addressed them in her own way. She used her platform to speak about the complexities of racial identity and the challenges faced by black artists. Though her performances were often misunderstood, Josephine viewed them as a form of resistance, a way of reclaiming and celebrating her identity.

In private, Josephine began to educate herself about African culture and history. She met with scholars and activists, deepening her understanding of the issues that shaped her heritage. This newfound knowledge influenced her art, and she began to incorporate themes of empowerment and resistance into her performances.

By the late 1920s, Josephine Baker had become one of the most sought-after performers in the world. She embarked on extensive tours across Europe, performing in cities such as Berlin, Vienna, and Milan. In each city, she was met with adoration, her shows selling out night after night.

One of the highlights of her European tour was her performance in Berlin. The city's vibrant nightlife and appreciation for avant-garde art made it the perfect backdrop for Josephine's daring style. Her shows in Berlin were electric, and her ability to captivate audiences transcended language and cultural barriers.

Josephine also made her way to South America, performing in Brazil and Argentina. Her energetic routines and magnetic presence won her fans across the continent, and she embraced the opportunity to learn about new cultures and musical traditions.

As her fame grew, Josephine had the opportunity to collaborate with some of the greatest artists of her time. She worked closely with choreographers, composers, and costume designers to refine her performances and elevate her artistry.

One of her most significant collaborations was with the French writer and director Georges Simenon, who helped her develop a cabaret show that blended humor, drama, and dance. This production showcased a more nuanced side of Josephine's talent, highlighting her ability to act as well as dance.

Josephine also collaborated with visual artists, including Pablo Picasso, who was fascinated by her energy and movement. Picasso sketched her on multiple occasions, capturing her essence in bold, abstract lines. These artistic partnerships not only enhanced Josephine's performances but also cemented her place in the broader cultural landscape of the Jazz Age.

For Josephine, Paris was more than just the city where she found fame it was a refuge from the racism and prejudice she had faced in the United States. In Paris, she was celebrated for her talent and individuality, not judged by the color of her skin. This acceptance allowed Josephine to flourish both professionally and personally.

She often spoke about the freedom she felt in Paris, describing it as a place where she could be herself without fear of judgment. This sense of liberation fueled her creativity and gave her the confidence to take risks in her art.

Paris also became the foundation for Josephine's philanthropy. She used her wealth and influence to support causes she believed in, including civil rights and education for underprivileged children. While her activism would become more prominent later in her life, the seeds of her philanthropic efforts were sown during her early years in Paris.

As the 1920s came to a close, Josephine Baker's career showed no signs of slowing down. She had firmly established herself as the Queen of Paris, a title she would carry for the rest of her life. Her performances continued to evolve, blending elements of music, dance, and theater to create experiences that were as innovative as they were entertaining.

Through her performances, Josephine redefined what it meant to be a black entertainer in the 20th century. She used her platform to celebrate her heritage, confront stereotypes, and inspire others to pursue their dreams, regardless of the obstacles they faced.

CHAPTER THREE

Josephine Baker And The Fight Against Racism

Josephine Baker's meteoric rise to fame in Europe had given her a platform few Black artists of her time could dream of. But beneath her dazzling performances and glamorous persona lay an unwavering determination to confront the systemic racism she had experienced firsthand. As an artist and an activist, Josephine's career became increasingly intertwined with her fight for racial equality, particularly in the United States.

In the 1930s, after years of stardom in Europe, Josephine Baker returned to the United States for a performance tour. Despite her international acclaim, she was met with the stark reality of racial segregation. American venues insisted on maintaining segregated seating arrangements, relegating Black patrons to the back of theaters or barring them entirely. For Josephine, this was a direct affront to her values.

She made it clear that she would not perform for segregated audiences. "I will not allow my art to be used as a tool to reinforce hatred," she declared. This stance cost her opportunities in some of the most prestigious venues in America. However, it also won her the admiration of civil rights organizations and Black communities across the country.

Josephine's insistence on equality wasn't just symbolic; it was revolutionary. At a time when many performers feared retaliation for speaking out, she risked her career to challenge the status quo. Her courage set an example for other artists and established her as a trailblazer in the fight against racism in the arts.

Josephine's advocacy for racial equality extended beyond her performances. She became an active supporter of the National Association for the

Advancement of Colored People (NAACP), one of the most prominent civil rights organizations in America. The NAACP recognized Josephine's influence and honored her with numerous awards for her contributions to the movement.

In 1951, the NAACP declared May 20th "Josephine Baker Day" in recognition of her tireless work for civil rights. On that day, Josephine delivered an impassioned speech at Carnegie Hall, where she addressed an audience of thousands. She spoke about her experiences with racism and urged Americans to confront the deep-seated prejudice that divided the nation.

Her words resonated with both Black and white audiences, inspiring many to join the fight for equality. Josephine's ability to connect with people from all walks of life was one of her greatest strengths as an activist. She used her fame not just to raise awareness but to bring people together in the struggle for justice.

Josephine's refusal to perform for segregated audiences wasn't limited to the United States. She took this principle with her wherever she went, demanding equality in every aspect of her career. In 1952, when she returned to perform at the Stork Club in New York, she confronted discrimination head-on. Despite being the headliner, she was refused service at the venue's restaurant. Josephine publicly denounced the incident, sparking a national conversation about racism in the entertainment industry.

This act of defiance was emblematic of Josephine's approach to activism. She was unafraid to speak out, even when it meant facing backlash from powerful institutions. Her willingness to challenge injustice inspired other artists to follow suit, gradually shifting the cultural landscape in America.

One of the most significant moments in Josephine Baker's activism came in 1963 when she participated in the March on Washington for Jobs and Freedom. This historic event brought together civil rights leaders, activists, and supporters to demand an end to racial discrimination and inequality.

Josephine was the only woman invited to speak at the event, a testament to her influence and stature within the movement. Wearing her French military uniform adorned with her wartime medals, she stood on the steps of the Lincoln Memorial and addressed the crowd.

In her speech, Josephine recounted her experiences as a Black woman who had faced discrimination in both her personal and professional life. She spoke about the progress that had been made but emphasized the need for continued action. "The fight is not over," she declared. "We must march forward until every child, regardless of color, has the same opportunities to dream and succeed.

Her words electrified the audience, many of whom had grown up watching her perform. Seeing Josephine use her platform to advocate for equality inspired a new generation of activists and solidified her place as a leader in the civil rights movement.

Josephine's commitment to racial equality wasn't confined to the United States. In Europe, she used her influence to challenge discriminatory practices and promote diversity. She performed benefit concerts to raise funds for anti-racism organizations and supported initiatives aimed at improving education and healthcare for underprivileged communities.

One of her most notable contributions was the establishment of her "Rainbow Tribe." This was Josephine's effort to demonstrate that people of all races and backgrounds could live together in harmony. She adopted twelve children from different countries, raising them at her château in France as a symbol of unity and love.

The Rainbow Tribe became a powerful statement against racism, challenging the notion of racial superiority and promoting the idea of global citizenship. Josephine's approach was both personal and political, blending her role as a mother with her mission as an activist.

Josephine Baker's role in the civil rights movement went beyond her public speeches and protests. Behind the scenes, she was a critical figure in providing resources and leveraging her influence to support the movement's leaders. During her trips to the United States, Josephine forged relationships with prominent civil rights figures, including Martin Luther King Jr., Rosa Parks, and Coretta Scott King. She became a confidante to many, using her global platform to amplify their voices.

Josephine's wealth and international connections proved to be invaluable. She quietly funded numerous civil rights initiatives, including voter registration drives and legal support for activists facing unjust imprisonment. While these efforts often went unpublicized, they were instrumental in sustaining the movement.

Her home in France became a meeting place for discussions about racial equality, as well as a safe haven for those who needed to regroup away from the constant threats of violence in the United States. Josephine understood the gravity of her role, and she saw herself not only as a symbol of change but as an active participant in making it happen.

Josephine's advocacy was met with widespread acclaim in Europe, but in her homeland, acceptance came slowly. Racism in the U.S. was deeply ingrained, and Josephine's outspoken nature made her a polarizing figure. While Black communities celebrated her, segments of white America saw her as a threat.

In 1951, when Josephine was denied service at the Stork Club in New York, she publicly exposed the racism she faced. The incident became a media firestorm, leading to a contentious legal battle. Josephine accused the club of racial discrimination, and while the case garnered significant attention, it also exposed her to harassment and threats.

This incident highlighted the challenges Josephine faced as a Black woman demanding equality in a segregated society. Unlike in Europe, where she was adored as an artist and a symbol of liberation, America presented constant hurdles, forcing her to confront the paradox of being a celebrated international star but marginalized in her own country.

Josephine's activism extended to using her art as a tool for change. She transformed her performances into statements against oppression, weaving messages of unity and resistance into her shows. Her iconic stage presence, adorned with dazzling costumes, became a symbol of defiance against the constraints of racism.

In her concerts, she often paused to speak directly to her audiences about the need for equality. These moments became some of the most powerful aspects of her performances, as she bridged the gap between entertainment and social activism. Her courage inspired other entertainers to use their platforms for advocacy, laying the groundwork for future generations of artist-activists.

During her U.S. tours, Josephine specifically targeted cities in the segregated South, where racial inequality was most pervasive. She demanded that venues desegregate their audiences or risk losing her performances. Many theaters, faced with the prospect of losing such a high-profile star, reluctantly complied, making Josephine one of the first artists to challenge segregation through her art.

In one notable instance, Josephine performed in Miami in 1951 to a fully integrated audience, a groundbreaking event in a city where segregation laws were strictly enforced. While this act of defiance drew criticism from white segregationists, it was a moment of hope and pride for the Black community, who saw it as a small but significant victory in the fight for equality.

While Josephine's work in the United States was crucial, her activism had a global reach. In South Africa during the apartheid era, Josephine refused to perform unless her shows were open to all races. Her demand sent shockwaves through the country, challenging a system that had institutionalized racial segregation.

Josephine also lent her voice to anti-colonial movements in Africa, supporting the fight for independence in countries like Algeria and Ghana. Her activism in these regions underscored her belief that the struggle for racial equality was not confined to one nation but was a global issue requiring collective action.

Josephine's unwavering commitment to justice came at a cost. She spent much of her fortune supporting civil rights causes, and her outspoken nature made her a target for surveillance and scrutiny. The FBI kept a file on her, viewing her activism as a potential threat during the height of McCarthyism.

Despite the financial strain and personal risks, Josephine remained undeterred. She believed that her success as an artist was meaningless if she didn't use it to fight for those who couldn't fight for themselves. Her determination was rooted in her own experiences of discrimination, which had shaped her understanding of the urgency of change.

In the final years of her life, Josephine continued to advocate for racial equality, even as her health began to decline. She participated in rallies, gave speeches, and maintained her efforts to desegregate performance venues. Her activism never wavered, and she remained a beacon of hope for those fighting against oppression.

Her dedication to the cause was evident until the very end. In her final public appearances, she reminded audiences that the fight for justice was ongoing. "We cannot rest," she often said. "The work is not done until freedom is a reality for all.

Josephine acknowledged these criticisms but refused to let them deter her. She continued to speak out against injustice, often at great personal cost. Her advocacy made her a target for government surveillance, and she was accused of being a communist during the height of the Red Scare.

Despite these obstacles, Josephine remained steadfast in her commitment to equality. She believed that her success as an artist came with a responsibility to use her platform for good.

CHAPTER FOUR

Josephine Baker And The French Resistance

When World War II erupted in 1939, Josephine Baker was already a household name in Europe, known for her electrifying performances and larger-than-life presence. She was living in France, a country that had embraced her as a star and where she had found a sense of belonging far removed from the racial prejudice of her native United States. But when Nazi Germany invaded France in 1940, her life took a dramatic turn.

Josephine, who had long admired France for its ideals of liberty, equality, and fraternity, could not stand idly by as her adopted homeland fell under occupation. Though she could have fled to safety, her sense of loyalty and justice propelled her toward a different path. She decided to join the fight against the Axis powers not as a soldier on the battlefield, but as a spy for the French Resistance.

Her fame, her charm, and her connections provided a unique opportunity. Josephine was an entertainer who could seamlessly move between the highest levels of European society, from diplomats to military officials, without raising suspicion. This made her an ideal operative for espionage.

Josephine's entry into the world of espionage began with Jacques Abtey, the head of French counterintelligence. Abtey, who was recruiting individuals for clandestine operations, recognized Josephine's potential immediately. Her ability to travel freely and mingle with influential figures in Europe meant she could gather information in places inaccessible to most spies.

Josephine didn't hesitate to offer her services. "France made me what I am," she reportedly said. "It is now my turn to help France." She officially became a member of the French Resistance, working under the guise of her glamorous public persona while secretly gathering critical intelligence.

Josephine's work as a spy often began on the stage. Her performances allowed her to travel extensively across Europe and North Africa, giving her the perfect cover for collecting and smuggling intelligence. She attended high-society parties, military gatherings, and embassy events, using her charm and wit to engage with officials and diplomats.

At these events, Josephine would listen closely to conversations, subtly steering discussions to extract valuable information about troop movements, supply routes, and enemy strategies. Her ability to speak multiple languages, including English, French, and German, gave her a significant advantage in her covert operations.

Josephine employed ingenious methods to transport the intelligence she gathered. She wrote notes in invisible ink on her sheet music or pinned them to the inside of her dresses. Sometimes, she memorized crucial details to avoid carrying any physical evidence. In one daring instance, she smuggled information written on her music sheets while traveling across borders. When searched by authorities, she played the role of an oblivious entertainer so convincingly that no one suspected her.

During the war, Josephine relocated to North Africa, where she used her estate in Morocco as a base for Resistance activities. The estate became a safe haven for Resistance members, a storage site for weapons and documents, and a meeting place for secret planning sessions. Josephine worked tirelessly, often hosting gatherings under the guise of social events to mask the covert activities happening behind the scenes.

In addition to her espionage work, Josephine provided material support to the Resistance. She used her wealth to buy supplies, vehicles, and communication equipment. She also took on the role of a recruiter, encouraging others to join the Resistance and fight against the Axis powers.

Josephine's work as a spy was fraught with danger. If caught, she would have faced imprisonment, torture, or execution at the hands of the Gestapo. Despite the risks, she remained steadfast in her mission. Her status as a beloved entertainer provided some protection, but it also made her a high-profile target.

At one point, Josephine fell seriously ill while in North Africa, suffering from an infection that required surgery. Even as she recovered, she continued her work for the Resistance, dictating messages and coordinating efforts from her hospital bed. Her unwavering commitment inspired those around her, reinforcing the importance of their mission.

Josephine's contributions did not go unnoticed. Her work provided the Allies with vital information that played a role in key military operations. Her ability to operate undetected in enemy territory made her an invaluable asset.

After the liberation of France in 1944, Josephine was recognized for her bravery and service. She was awarded the Croix de Guerre and the Rosette de la Résistance, two of France's highest military honors. Later, she was made a Chevalier of the Legion of Honor by Charles de Gaulle, cementing her legacy as a war hero.

Josephine Baker's work with the French Resistance showcased a different side of the star who had dazzled audiences with her banana skirt and captivating performances. In the fight against fascism, she demonstrated that courage, loyalty, and resilience could triumph over fear and oppression.

Her contributions to the war effort went beyond espionage. Josephine's very existence as a Black woman working against Nazi Germany was a statement of defiance. She shattered stereotypes and proved that anyone, regardless of race or gender, could play a critical role in the fight for freedom.

What made Josephine's story particularly remarkable was her ability to balance her dual identities. By day, she was the glamorous entertainer, adored by millions; by night, she was a spy risking her life for the cause of liberty. This duality was not without its challenges, but Josephine navigated both worlds with remarkable finesse.

Josephine Baker's career as a spy during World War II was filled with near-misses and moments of extraordinary danger. One of the most harrowing aspects of her work involved traveling across war-torn Europe and North Africa while carrying classified information. Every border crossing was a potential trap, with Nazi guards meticulously inspecting travelers for signs of espionage. Josephine, ever the performer, relied on her charm and wit to disarm suspicion.

In one particularly daring instance, Josephine attended a high-profile party hosted by Nazi collaborators. This event was a calculated risk; the gathering included German officers, local sympathizers, and European dignitaries. While mingling, Josephine eavesdropped on conversations, memorizing critical details about troop movements and supply lines. Despite the oppressive atmosphere, she remained calm, masking her unease with her signature charisma. That night, she left the event with vital intelligence that would later be smuggled to Allied forces.

The act of memorizing information became one of Josephine's most valuable skills. When the risk of carrying physical documents was too high, she committed details to memory, often encoding them in song lyrics or poetry. This creative method not only protected her but ensured that vital intelligence reached its destination.

Josephine Baker's success as a spy was partly due to her ability to blend into diverse social environments. She adapted her public persona to suit the context, whether performing for Allied soldiers or attending diplomatic events. Her wardrobe became a critical tool in her espionage work, as she used costumes and accessories to conceal documents and other items.

On one occasion, Josephine wore a dress with hidden compartments sewn into the lining. Within these compartments were maps and letters intended for the Resistance. Her flamboyant outfits drew admiration but also served as an ingenious form of misdirection.

When Nazi guards conducted inspections, they were often too distracted by her star power to thoroughly search her belongings.

In addition to disguising physical items, Josephine adopted various personas. She could be the enchanting entertainer, the humble humanitarian, or the outspoken activist, depending on the situation. This adaptability made her one of the most effective spies in the French Resistance, capable of infiltrating spaces others could not.

While Josephine's primary role in the Resistance was gathering intelligence, her contributions extended far beyond espionage. She used her international platform to raise funds for the Free French Forces, performing concerts to generate support for the war effort. These events, often held in neutral territories, provided critical financial resources for the Resistance and boosted morale among Allied troops.

Josephine's charitable work also included providing aid to refugees and displaced persons. She opened her home in Morocco to those fleeing the horrors of war, offering shelter, food, and safety. Her estate became a hub of activity, with people from all walks of life finding solace in her generosity.

Her efforts did not go unnoticed. Letters of gratitude poured in from soldiers, Resistance members, and civilians who had been touched by her kindness. For many, Josephine Baker was not just a spy or a performer but a symbol of hope in a world darkened by conflict.

Josephine's work brought her into contact with some of the most influential figures of the Allied war effort. She developed close relationships with military officials, diplomats, and intelligence operatives, using these connections to further the Resistance's goals. One notable ally was General Charles de Gaulle, leader of the Free French Forces, who deeply admired Josephine's bravery and patriotism.

In her collaboration with Allied intelligence agencies, Josephine often served as a liaison, facilitating the exchange of information between different groups. Her multilingual abilities and international reputation allowed her to bridge gaps between Resistance cells operating in different regions. This coordination was crucial in ensuring the success of key missions.

One of Josephine Baker's most significant contributions to the war effort took place in Casablanca, Morocco, during the Allied conferences held in 1943. These meetings, attended by figures like Winston Churchill and Franklin D. Roosevelt, shaped the course of the war. Josephine, though not an official participant, played a behind-the-scenes role in supporting the event.

Through her performances and social engagements, Josephine gathered intelligence on the movements of Axis forces in North Africa. She also helped organize logistics for Resistance members operating in the region. Her work during this period underscored her ability to blend artistry with activism, using every opportunity to further the cause of freedom.

By the end of World War II, Josephine Baker had risked her life countless times for the French Resistance. The war left her physically and emotionally exhausted, but she emerged as a hero, celebrated for her courage and sacrifice. Her contributions were formally recognized with numerous accolades, including the Médaille de la Résistance and the Legion of Honor.

Despite her accolades, Josephine rarely spoke about her wartime experiences in detail. For her, the work was not about seeking recognition but about fulfilling a moral obligation. She carried the memories of her espionage work with quiet pride, knowing she had played a part in shaping the course of history.

Josephine Baker's role in the French Resistance is a testament to her extraordinary character. She defied expectations and stereotypes, proving that a Black woman, born into poverty in the segregated United States, could become a global icon and a war hero.

Her work as a spy highlighted her intelligence, resourcefulness, and bravery, qualities that defined her throughout her life. In the face of immense danger, she chose to fight for a cause greater than herself, leaving an indelible mark on history.

Even during the war, Josephine found ways to use her art as a form of resistance. She continued to perform for Allied troops, boosting morale and reminding them of what they were fighting for. Her shows often included patriotic themes, reinforcing the ideals of freedom and unity.

In the years following the war, Josephine spoke openly about her experiences, ensuring that the sacrifices of the Resistance were not forgotten. She became a symbol of resilience, a reminder that even in the darkest of times, individuals have the power to make a difference.

CHAPTER FIVE

A Mother To The World

Josephine Baker's extraordinary life was not only defined by her artistry, activism, and espionage but also by her remarkable vision of building a family that embodied her ideals of racial harmony and unity. In the aftermath of World War II, Josephine turned her attention to a new dream: the creation of what she called the "Rainbow Tribe."

This vision stemmed from Josephine's deep desire to counteract the divisions of race, religion, and nationality that plagued society. Having grown up in a racially segregated America and witnessed the horrors of bigotry across the globe, Josephine sought to prove that people of all races and cultures could live together in harmony. Her plan was ambitious and unconventional for its time: she would adopt children from different ethnic backgrounds and raise them as siblings in a loving, inclusive environment.

Josephine's dream was not merely an act of charity; it was a profound statement against the prejudices that divided humanity. She believed that her family could serve as a living example of unity, showing the world that love and acceptance could transcend the barriers of race and culture.

In the late 1940s and early 1950s, Josephine began putting her dream into action. Her first adoption was Akio, a Japanese boy she met during a visit to Japan. Moved by his story and the devastation of war that had affected so many children, Josephine decided to bring Akio into her family. This act marked the beginning of what would become her most personal and ambitious project.

To house her growing family and bring her vision of the Rainbow Tribe to life, Josephine purchased the Château des Milandes, a stunning castle in the French countryside. The estate became the heart of her experiment in global harmony. Josephine transformed the château into a sanctuary, complete with lush gardens, playgrounds, and classrooms designed to nurture her children's education and development.

The daily life at Château des Milandes was as unique as Josephine herself. Each child was encouraged to embrace their cultural heritage while learning about the traditions and histories of their siblings' backgrounds. Josephine hired tutors and staff from around the world to provide a well-rounded education, emphasizing tolerance and understanding. She believed that by exposing her children to diverse perspectives, she could instill in them the values of empathy and mutual respect.

Despite her busy schedule as a performer and activist, Josephine was deeply involved in her children's lives. She made it a priority to spend time with them, whether it was through shared meals, storytelling, or celebrating cultural festivals from their respective homelands. Her efforts to create a harmonious and loving environment were driven by her unwavering belief in the power of family as a microcosm of society.

While Josephine's vision for the Rainbow Tribe was groundbreaking, it was not without its challenges. Raising twelve children from different cultural backgrounds in a single household presented logistical and emotional hurdles. The children often faced scrutiny and prejudice from outsiders who questioned the legitimacy of Josephine's unconventional family.

Critics accused Josephine of using her children as a "publicity stunt" or an idealized symbol of her beliefs. Some argued that her approach to parenting was too idealistic, pointing out that her demanding career often took her away from home for extended periods. There were also financial difficulties; maintaining the château and providing for such a large family proved to be an immense burden, especially as Josephine's earnings from her performances began to dwindle in her later years.

Despite these challenges, Josephine remained steadfast in her commitment to the Rainbow Tribe. She defended her family against criticism, emphasizing that her intentions were rooted in love and a genuine desire to promote peace and understanding.

Josephine's efforts to build the Rainbow Tribe extended beyond her immediate family. She used the château as a cultural and educational center, inviting visitors from around the world to witness her vision in action. She believed that by showcasing her family's unity, she could inspire others to embrace the ideals of racial harmony and coexistence.

Public tours of the château became a way for Josephine to share her message with a wider audience. Visitors were greeted with performances, exhibitions, and cultural displays that highlighted the beauty of diversity. Josephine's children often participated in these events, serving as ambassadors of her vision.

The Rainbow Tribe also became a focal point of Josephine's activism. She frequently spoke about her family in interviews, emphasizing the importance of breaking down racial barriers and fostering understanding. Her message resonated with audiences around the world, further cementing her legacy as a champion of equality.

Josephine Baker's role as a mother to the Rainbow Tribe was not only a reflection of her dreams but also of her innate maternal instincts. She approached parenting with profound emotional depth, striving to create a nurturing environment for her children. To Josephine, each child was unique, and she tailored her care to address their individual needs.

Josephine was known for her creativity in how she bonded with her children. She organized storytelling nights where she narrated tales from different cultures, intertwining elements of history, folklore, and moral lessons. Her stories were not merely bedtime entertainment but tools to broaden her children's perspectives and instill in them a sense of pride in their heritage.

She also celebrated each child's cultural background through special rituals. On birthdays, Josephine would cook or arrange meals inspired by the child's native cuisine, turning these celebrations into opportunities for the entire family to learn about and appreciate one another's cultures. This attention to detail and her ability to make every child feel valued strengthened the bonds within her family.

Life at Château des Milandes was far from ordinary, yet Josephine was adamant about instilling discipline and strong moral values in her children. She believed that a structured routine was essential for their growth, especially given the media attention and societal challenges they often faced as part of her unconventional family.

Each morning began with a family breakfast, where Josephine encouraged discussions about kindness, tolerance, and current events. It was her way of ensuring that her children developed critical thinking skills and compassion. Afterward, the children attended classes with tutors, learning not only standard subjects but also languages, music, and art. Josephine was especially passionate about the arts, viewing them as a universal language that could bridge cultural divides.

Afternoons often involved outdoor activities, from gardening to playing sports, which Josephine believed fostered teamwork and a connection to nature. Evening meals were communal, serving as a time to reflect on the day's lessons and reinforce the importance of family unity.

While Josephine's vision for the Rainbow Tribe was grand, the financial reality of maintaining such a large family and the Château des Milandes often weighed heavily on her. She poured much of her personal earnings into the upkeep of the château, education for her children, and ensuring they had access to the best opportunities available.

As her career entered its later stages, Josephine faced declining income, which made it increasingly difficult to sustain her ambitious vision. She was forced to take on additional performances and tours, even when her health began to falter. Her unwavering commitment to her family often came at a personal cost, as she prioritized their well-being over her own.

Despite these challenges, Josephine remained resourceful. She opened the château to tourists, hosting cultural festivals and performances to generate income. She also sought financial support from patrons who admired her work and shared her belief in the ideals of equality and unity.

The Rainbow Tribe's story would not be complete without considering the perspectives of Josephine's children, many of whom have spoken about their experiences in later years. While they cherished the unique upbringing their mother provided, they also acknowledged the complexities of growing up in such a public and idealized family.

Some children described the immense pressure they felt to live up to Josephine's vision, as they were often viewed as symbols rather than individuals. They faced scrutiny from outsiders and struggled to navigate their identities in a world that was not always accepting of their family's diversity.

Nevertheless, they also expressed deep gratitude for the values Josephine instilled in them. Her lessons on love, tolerance, and cultural pride left a lasting impact, shaping their outlook on life and relationships. For many, the Rainbow Tribe was not just a family but a testament to the power of unity and resilience.

Josephine's work with the Rainbow Tribe extended beyond her family and into the realm of global activism. She used her platform as an international star to advocate for children's rights and racial equality. She partnered with organizations to raise awareness about issues affecting children around the world, from poverty to access to education.

One notable moment came when Josephine addressed the United Nations, sharing her vision for a world where children of all backgrounds could thrive without fear of discrimination. Her speech, though brief, was powerful and echoed the values she lived by every day as the matriarch of the Rainbow Tribe.

In addition to her advocacy work, Josephine was involved in efforts to support orphans and displaced children in war-torn regions. She often donated money and resources to organizations that aligned with her mission, further solidifying her legacy as a humanitarian.

As Josephine Baker's life neared its later years, the Rainbow Tribe remained a central part of her identity. Even as financial hardships forced her to leave the Château des Milandes, her children stood by her, a testament to the enduring bond she had cultivated within her family.

Josephine encouraged her children to view their diversity as a source of strength. She often reminded them that they were part of something larger than themselves a family that represented the possibility of a better, more inclusive world.

Her guidance and example instilled in them a deep sense of pride in their identities and their role in carrying forward her legacy.

CHAPTER SIX

The Comeback Josephine Baker's Return To The Stage

By the 1950s, Josephine Baker was a name etched in the annals of history a trailblazing entertainer, a war hero, and an advocate for equality. Yet, the golden threads of her life had begun to fray. Financial troubles loomed, threatening to overshadow her legacy. But Baker, resilient and ever-defiant, was far from finished. This chapter chronicles her struggle to regain her footing on the stage, her indomitable spirit in the face of adversity, and her enduring fight for justice during the Civil Rights Movement.

After World War II, Josephine's life took a turn that few could have anticipated. Despite her decorated service as a member of the French Resistance and her international acclaim, her personal finances were in dire straits. Lavish spending on her estate, Château des Milandes, coupled with her commitment to supporting her "Rainbow Tribe" of adopted children, left her financially strained. She poured resources into making her château a symbol of unity and acceptance, hosting visitors from around the world to witness her vision of racial harmony.

However, the upkeep of the château was costly, and Josephine's income dwindled. Concert tours became infrequent, and she struggled to adapt to an entertainment industry increasingly dominated by younger stars and changing tastes. By 1951, she faced mounting debts, and foreclosure loomed over her beloved estate. Yet, Josephine refused to succumb to despair. She was determined to reclaim her position as an icon, not just for herself, but for the values she championed.

Josephine's comeback began in earnest in 1952, fueled by a hunger to prove her enduring relevance. She embarked on a series of performances across Europe and the United States, reinventing herself as a timeless performer. She retained the vivacity of her earlier years but imbued her shows with a newfound depth, blending her signature charm with poignant reflections on the racial struggles of the era.

Her return to America marked a turning point. Initially, she faced resistance from venues unwilling to challenge the entrenched segregation of the time. Yet, Josephine was resolute: she would only perform in integrated settings. In 1951, she made headlines when she performed at the Stork Club in New York, where she boldly criticized the venue for its discriminatory practices. This public stand against racism cemented her status as more than just an entertainer it reaffirmed her as a warrior for justice.

Her efforts paid off. In 1953, she returned to Paris, where her performances at the Olympia Theatre were met with rapturous applause. Critics hailed her as a symbol of resilience and artistry, with reviews celebrating her ability to captivate audiences of all ages. Josephine's star had not dimmed it had evolved.

Even as she reclaimed her position in the spotlight, Josephine remained deeply committed to the fight for equality. The Civil Rights Movement in the United States reached a fever pitch during the 1950s and 1960s, and Josephine lent her voice and influence to the cause. Her speeches were as powerful as her performances, resonating with those who sought an ally in their struggle for justice.

In 1963, she joined Dr. Martin Luther King Jr. during the historic March on Washington, standing before thousands at the Lincoln Memorial. Draped in her French military uniform adorned with medals from her wartime service, Josephine delivered a heartfelt speech. "I have walked into the palaces of kings and queens and into the houses of presidents," she declared, "but I could not walk into a hotel in America and get a cup of coffee." Her words electrified the crowd, a poignant reminder of the systemic injustices she had faced and the progress yet to be made.

Josephine's activism extended beyond the stage. She participated in protests, fundraisers, and advocacy campaigns, leveraging her fame to amplify the voices of the oppressed. Her dual identity as a global superstar and an impassioned activist made her a bridge between worlds, uniting audiences and inspiring change.

The 1960s saw Josephine embraced as a cultural icon once more. Her performances became celebratory affairs, drawing diverse crowds eager to witness a legend in her element. In 1969, she performed at Carnegie Hall, receiving a standing ovation that brought her to tears. It was a moment of vindication a testament to her enduring relevance and the love of an audience that had never forgotten her.

CHAPTER SEVEN

Josephine Baker's Enduring Impact

Josephine Baker's life was extraordinary not just in what she achieved during her lifetime but in the lasting legacy she left behind. As an artist, activist, and humanitarian, she carved out a path few dared to tread, and her story continues to resonate across cultures and generations. From her induction into the Panthéon to the influence she has wielded in art, civil rights, and global humanitarian efforts, Josephine Baker's impact remains profound.

Josephine Baker's artistic contributions redefined the possibilities for Black performers in the 20th century. From the moment she first took the stage in the 1920s, she shattered stereotypes and challenged conventions. Her fearless embrace of her identity as both a Black woman and an entertainer captivated audiences worldwide and paved the way for future generations of artists of color.

Her groundbreaking debut in La Revue Nègre in Paris in 1925 was not merely a spectacle but a turning point. Her provocative performances, such as the iconic Danse Sauvage, became emblematic of the Jazz Age, while her ability to blend humor, sensuality, and dance earned her a place in the pantheon of global entertainment. Even after her prime, her artistry continued to inspire younger performers like Eartha Kitt, Nina Simone, and later Beyoncé women who saw in Josephine an example of unapologetic self-expression and cultural pride.

Josephine's artistic influence extended beyond performance. She redefined what it meant to be a global superstar. Her work with leading choreographers, designers, and musicians expanded the possibilities for collaboration in the performing arts. Her signature banana skirt became a symbol of cultural reclamation, a motif reinterpreted by artists and designers as an emblem of empowerment rather than objectification.

Josephine Baker's activism during her lifetime set her apart from her peers. Her tireless commitment to social justice and equality has become an enduring part of her legacy. Long before it was fashionable or even safe to speak out, she leveraged her fame to advocate for racial and social equality.

During the Civil Rights Movement, her defiance of racial segregation in the United States inspired a generation of activists. Her demand for integrated audiences during her U.S. tours in the 1950s and her visible presence alongside Dr. Martin Luther King Jr. at the 1963 March on Washington positioned her as a critical ally in the fight for civil rights. She used her platform to challenge institutions, even risking her career by boycotting venues that refused to adopt inclusive policies.

Baker's activism wasn't confined to speeches and symbolic gestures. Her adoption of 12 children from diverse racial and ethnic backgrounds whom she referred to as her "Rainbow Tribe" embodied her vision of a world free of prejudice. She believed her family could serve as a living example of racial harmony, an aspiration that remains relevant to modern discussions of diversity and inclusion.

Her advocacy extended to her work with refugees and displaced individuals after World War II. Baker's support for humanitarian causes laid the groundwork for the intersection of celebrity and activism, inspiring subsequent generations of artists like Harry Belafonte, Sidney Poitier, and later, Angelina Jolie, to use their platforms for meaningful social change.

Josephine Baker's humanitarian legacy goes beyond the Civil Rights Movement. Her work during World War II, serving as a spy and courier for the French Resistance, demonstrated her willingness to risk her life for a greater cause. She leveraged her fame to gather intelligence, transport documents, and provide moral support to Allied troops. Her bravery earned her the Croix de Guerre and the Rosette de la Résistance, as well as the distinction of being the first American-born woman to receive full French military honors at her funeral.

Beyond her wartime efforts, Baker's philanthropy shaped her global impact. She used her resources to create opportunities for others, often at great personal cost. The financial struggles she endured later in life were a testament to her unwavering generosity, as she prioritized the well-being of others over her own material comfort.

Her work with the International League Against Racism and Anti-Semitism further solidified her role as a humanitarian. Josephine wasn't content to address only one issue; she saw the interconnectedness of oppression and sought to combat injustice wherever it arose. This holistic approach to activism has inspired modern movements that emphasize intersectionality in the fight for equality.

In 2021, nearly half a century after her passing, Josephine Baker achieved an honor befitting her monumental contributions to the world. She was inducted into the Panthéon in Paris, France's highest posthumous distinction, reserved for individuals who have made extraordinary contributions to the nation's history and culture.

The ceremony was a celebration of her multifaceted legacy. Her voice echoed through the corridors of the Panthéon as recordings of her songs played, reminding the world of her dual identity as an entertainer and activist. Her induction also served as a recognition of her contributions to France during its darkest hours, as well as her lifelong fight for justice and equality.

Josephine's induction was a landmark moment for women, Black individuals, and immigrants. She became the first Black woman and one of the few women overall to be enshrined in the Panthéon. This recognition symbolized not only her extraordinary life but also France's evolving acknowledgment of its multicultural identity. Her legacy as a symbol of resilience, courage, and compassion was immortalized in one of the most revered spaces in French history.

Josephine Baker's story continues to inspire. Her fearless pursuit of justice and equality resonates with activists and artists alike. Modern performers cite her as a source of creative and personal inspiration, and her life has been the subject of countless books, documentaries, and films.

Her example has also influenced the way celebrities engage with social and political causes. Figures like Oprah Winfrey, Rihanna, and Zendaya have drawn on Baker's model of using fame as a platform for advocacy. The ethos of inclusivity and cultural pride that defined her career has found new life in contemporary discussions about representation and equity in the arts.

Josephine's legacy also lives on in education. Schools, foundations, and cultural institutions around the world continue to honor her contributions. Scholarships and programs inspired by her life promote the arts and activism, ensuring that her spirit of generosity and courage endures.

Josephine Baker's enduring impact is a testament to the power of art, activism, and humanity. Her life was a bridge between worlds Black and white, American and French, entertainer and freedom fighter. She refused to be confined by societal expectations, creating a legacy that transcends time and geography.

As the first Black woman enshrined in the Panthéon, she stands as a symbol of progress, reminding the world of the importance of inclusivity and equality. Her story continues to inspire those who dare to dream of a better world, one where courage and compassion can break down even the most entrenched barriers.

Printed in Dunstable, United Kingdom